Fast Cash

9 Amazing Ways To Make Money

Without Having To Work At A Job

By

Omar Johnson

© Copyright 2013. Make Profits Easy LLC

Table of Contents

Introduction 3

Chapter 1: How To Make Fast Cash as a Consultant 6

Chapter 2: How To Make Fast Cash with Affiliate Marketing 14

Chapter 3: How to Make Fast Cash Selling on E-Bay 21

Chapter 4: How To Make Fast Cash through Amazon's Associates Program 28

Chapter 5: How To Make Fast Cash Selling eBooks 35

Chapter 6: How To Make Fast Cash Publishing Kindle Books on Amazon 41

Chapter 7: How To Make Fast Cash by Offering Small Services on Fiverr.Com 49

Chapter 8: How To Make Fast Cash Mystery Shopping 54

Chapter 9: How To Make Fast Cash Flipping Websites 61

Introduction

This book has caught your attention mainly because you are highly interested in knowing how to make money without having to work at a job. Perhaps you presently work at a job and are looking for creative ways to make additional income without having to take a second job or perhaps you just don't like working for someone else and you want to strike out on your own. Your situation may even be that you are currently unemployed.

Whatever your particular case maybe, the bottom line is that you need to make money fast! **Fast Cash** will help you achieve that goal by revealing to you 9 amazing ways that you can utilize to make money without having to work at a job.

What You'll Learn

Each Fast Cash money method mentioned here is user-friendly, doesn't require a lot of start-up capital, and can provide you with money in your pocket instantly. Here is an overview of the different types of money making methods that you should expect to learn about:

1. How to make Fast Cash with affiliate marketing
2. How to make Fast Cash selling on E-Bay
3. How to make Fast Cash through Amazon's Associates Program
4. How to make Fast Cash selling E-Books on your website and other venues
5. How to make Fast Cash publishing Kindle books on Amazon
6. How to make Fast Cash by offering small services on Fiverr.Com
7. How to make Fast Cash mystery shopping
8. How to make Fast Cash flipping websites
9. How to make Fast Cash as a consultant

In each section, we'll provide you with practical tips that you can use to start making money with each one of these methods.

How Much Will You Earn?

The concepts that we speak about in this book should provide you with enough knowledge to earn anywhere from $200 to $5,000 per month (or more). The amount that you make specifically will be directly correlated with how quickly you pick up the information as well as how accurately you apply it. If you remain consistent, you should start seeing your efforts pay off in little to no time at all.

Chapter 1: How To Make Fast Cash as a Consultant

Offering your services as a consultant is a simple and easy way to put fast cash in your pocket. Many people both online and offline need help from individuals who have specialized knowledge in different areas to assist them in carrying out their daily tasks and reaching their goals and objectives. As a consultant you will offer these types of services to them.

Creating a Consulting Business Based On Your Skill Set And Expertise

To determine what type of consulting services you should offer, you should first examine your present skill set. What do you presently do well or you're an expert at that you can offer as a service to others? For example, are you a great writer and knowledgeable and adept at business? If so you can create and offer a consulting service that entails writing business proposals and business plans for startups.

If you are an expert at Photoshop you can offer consulting services to people that need artsy type of things done for them which they have no clue about like logo design or creating a fabulous book cover. The possibilities can be endless and to get started all you would have to do is assess what you do best or you're an expert at and create a consulting service around it if it makes sense and it is commercially viable.

You Don't Have To Be An Expert

But what if you're not expert at anything can you still be a consultant? The answer is a resounding yes! All you would have to do is cheaply outsource the work to others who are experts at what they do and create a consulting business behind it. For example, let's say that you wanted to be a social media consultant but you knew very little about how to build a business Twitter page or a Facebook business page, you can simply outsource this task to someone who does.

In fact, social media management is in such in high demand these days because business owners large and small want a strong social media presence so that they could gain new customers and keep in contact with past customers that if you decide to create a consultant business in this area you will profit immensely.

Here is a brief list of some of the consultant services that you can offer to business owners by outsourcing the tasks associated with them.

- SEO
- Blog Design and Management
- Website Design
- Mobile Marketing Assistance
- Reputation Management

Here are some tips that you should consider implementing when creating your consulting business:

- **Sell results, not services** – The bottom line is people want results so sell them on the results that you can achieve for them. Yes, tell them about your services but what they really want to hear is something more meaningful and specific like "I can guarantee that I will get you 3,000 Twitter followers in your local area within the next 30 days". Taking this approach will help you immensely in closing the deal. However, once the deal is signed and sealed you have to deliver on your promises or your credibility will suffer.

- **Distinguish yourself from your competitors** - You have to differentiate yourself from your competitors or you will be viewed as a commodity. When you are viewed as a commodity and similar to everyone else people will always choose the person that is offering the lowest price for their services.

- **Knowing your pricing structure** - You should be prepared to quote a price when people ask the question "what do you charge for the variety of services that you offer "The answer should roll right off your tongue without hesitation.

- **Marketing your consulting services** – In order to drum up business it is essential that you market your consulting services to the marketplace. Marketing is the fuel that drives the engine in your consultant business.

  You can market and promote your consulting services to local business owners via direct mail using letters, flyers, brochures etc. Or you can market your services through freelancer hubs such as elance.com, odesk.com, guru.com or freelancer.com. You can also market your consulting services on E-Bay as well.

  Now that you know that marketing your consultant business is the key to your success to making fast cash, you need to create the marketing materials that will attract potential customers by the boatload.

"Done For You" "Ready To Use" Marketing Materials To Attract Customers For Your Consultant Business

Before you start panicking and thinking "wow that sounds like a lot of work" I actually made it easy for you by creating a "done for you" marketing system that can turn your local business prospects into paying customers. I call that marketing system "The Local Customer Connection Pack".

The Local Customer Connection package will help you soft-sell your services to local business owners by helping them understand WHY online marketing is the perfect way to "Connect" with local customers. This content simply educates them about the different marketing methods available to them and HOW it can help them generate NEW and REPEAT business.

The following represents some of the topics that are covered in this package:

- Attract Local Customers with Search Engine Visibility (Google Places, SEO, and More)
- Attract Local Customers with a Profitable Website
- Attract Local Customers with Email Marketing
- Attract Local Customers with Mobile Marketing
- Attract Local Customers with Social Media
- Attract Local Customers with Video Marketing
- Attract Local Customers with Online Content Creation & Distribution
- Attract Local Customers with Online Reputation Management
- Attract Local Customers with Online Classified Ads
- Attract Local Customers with Paid Online Advertising

What's even more incredible is that you can even brand this package with your own information and then give it away to generate leads or even sell it outright to local business owners. Trust me I've saved you blood, sweat and tears by simply handing you this amazing "done for you" marketing system on a silver platter. To gain access to this super marketing system just visit the following link:

http://www.gmapleadgenerator.com/lcc.html

Conclusion:

There are a great deal of people in the marketplace who are looking for and value what a knowledgeable consultant has to offer. If you position and market yourself properly to this particular audience you will capitalize profit wise on this demand and need that exists.

Remember to assess your present skill set to determine what you have to immediately offer to this target audience, but also remember if you are unable to find any particular skill set that may be of value to others in yourself you can still create a consultant business by simply outsourcing tasks to others while you take the credit this is perfectly normal and will put you on the road to fast cash as a consultant in no time.

Chapter 2: How To Make Fast Cash with Affiliate Marketing

In short, affiliate marketing is the act of promoting products or services in return for a certain commission. Depending on how effectively you do this, there is a chance that you could earn anywhere from a few hundred to a few thousand dollars each and every month. Sure, being a big-time affiliate marketer can be very profitable and even fun, but how can you break into this field and start making money right away? That's what we'll discuss in this chapter.

What You Should Know About Affiliate Marketing

As we previously mentioned, you'll have the opportunity to earn thousands and thousands of dollars each and every month from affiliate marketing. However, you do need to keep in mind that it involves driving a good amount of traffic to your website or blog in order to accomplish this. The process works quite simply: whenever a visitor clicks on an affiliate-sponsored ad, they will be sent to your merchant's company website.

Depending on how the pay structure works, you'll either get paid for that click on your affiliate link or get paid whenever that visitor makes a purchase through your affiliate link. You'll generally receive a commission on whatever is sold. While it may sound difficult, the truth is that you can set-up your own affiliate marketing website in a matter of days and start making money shortly after. Here are a few of the benefits associated with affiliate marketing:

- No stock or inventory.
- Opportunity to make thousands of dollars each month.
- Simple to set-up and maintain.
- Can be repeated over and over again.

Today, affiliate marketing is quite common and it's certainly possible to make significant profits as long as you know what you're doing. Here are some tips to ensure that you are on the right track.

Tips for Succeeding With Affiliate Marketing

First off, it is very important that you drive in massive amounts of traffic to your website or blog. Traffic is the key to succeeding with affiliate marketing and a lack of it will result in little to no profits. Also make sure that you are only associating yourself with reputable and professional affiliate marketing programs. Otherwise, you'll risk losing loyal followers. Here are a few more tips to consider for succeeding with affiliate marketing:

- **High-Commission Payouts**: Search for an affiliate program that is going to reward you with a relatively high percentage of any sales that you help make. For instance, if you're making 50% of every sale that you promote then chances are good that you'll be able to earn several thousand dollars per month. On the flipside, this can be difficult to do if you're only making 10% of every sale.

- **Promote Quality Products**: Would you purchase or use the product that you're promoting? If your answer is "No" then you need to consider choosing another product to promote. Remember that long-term success in affiliate marketing boils down to promoting quality products. This will ensure that you build trust with your followers and that they keep coming back.

- **Create a Website or Blog**: Probably the easiest way to make money with affiliate marketing is to create a website or blog around your particular niche. For instance, if you're selling motorcycle parts as an affiliate marketer then you should consider starting up a motorcycle-related website. This will provide you with a simple and effective platform for making money with affiliate marketing.

One of the biggest mistakes that affiliate marketers make is not properly blending in their links with their content. But you need to make sure that you are not doing this deceptively. Overall, you want your site pages to flow smoothly but you also want to make sure that you're incorporating relevant links to the products or services that you're promoting. Keep in mind that you'll be using banner ads to promote companies in certain cases.

Increasing Revenues - Strategies to Consider

Making money with affiliate marketing is one thing, but making a lot of money can be another. If you're truly interested in making a significant amount of money through affiliate marketing then you should consider a few things. One strategy that you can try implementing is using Google Ad Words as a way of driving additional traffic to your website or blog.

Note that this does require a small investment so you need to make sure that you're approaching it correctly. The best thing you can do is to experiment with different budgets and keywords until you find the one that is most profitable for the products that you're promoting. When setting up an Ad Words advertising box, make sure that you include the following:

- Name of your website.

- Link to your website.
- Product or service that you're promoting.
- Brief description of what you're offering.

You can start advertising with as little as $10 and slowly increase this amount once you have figured out a keyword combination that works. Some of the more successful affiliate marketers are well-known for being able to leverage Google Ad Words in a manner that drives in the most amount of traffic possible.

How Long Does it Take to Make Money?

Affiliate marketing is a money making method that can earn you a significant amount of money in a relatively short amount of time. As a general rule of thumb, the amount of money that you earn will be directly correlated with the amount of demand and competition associated with what you're promoting. If you can find a product or service that is in high demand but that poses little competition then you'll stand a better chance of making a lot of money on a monthly basis.

Conclusion

Overall, the chances of making money with affiliate marketing are relatively high, as long as you follow the tips and strategies presented here. For people with little to no money, affiliate marketing can be a great way to make money without a job. Just make sure that you're promoting relevant and high-quality products so that you don't lose followers.

Chapter 3: How to Make Fast Cash Selling on E-Bay

Why has making money on E-Bay become so appealing, especially for those who seek to strike out on their own? Aside from being quite fun, selling on E-Bay can prove to be quite profitable as long as you follow a few key principles. And what if you're someone who is interested in selling more than a few items? Is there a way to turn this model into a profitable business? In this chapter, we are going to discuss that.

Overview - How to Be Successful on E-Bay

Being successful on E-Bay requires that you do a lot of research in terms of what is trending and what is not, the pricing of items, the evaluating of the competition etc. Fortunately, this is a business structure that can provide you with the opportunity to start making money right away. Starting out, one could expect to earn anywhere from a few hundred to a few thousand dollars per month. But once you start building up a reputation on E-Bay, it can be quite easy to sell tens of thousands of dollars' worth of items on a monthly basis.

How to Research Products

Probably one of the best strategies that you can utilize is to start doing thorough amounts of research on the various products that you're interested in selling. This will ultimately tell you the price at which you should sell your item so that you can gain maximum value for it. Here are a few questions that you should be asking yourself while partaking in product research:

- Is there a market for this particular product?
- How much money is this product really worth?
- How much competition am I going to go up against?
- How sustainable is this product for the long-term?

Answering these questions can be really helpful. They will provide you with important information regarding how you should price your product and your listing strategy. Remember that in some cases, it may not even be worth your time to sell an item. Make sure that you answer each of these questions before proceeding with selling any item.

What You Should Know About Shipping

Believe it or not, shipping will play a huge role in how much you actually make on E-Bay. Aside from making sure that your products are easy to ship, you need to make sure that they aren't too expensive to send to customers. For instance, are you going to spend $50 (or more) for international shipping for a $5 product? This would be foolish and would only negatively impact your success. If possible, try to focus on products that have a lot of value, that are easy to ship, and aren't expensive to package and send.

Writing Product Descriptions

As someone who would like to make money selling items on E-Bay, it is critical that you learn how to write captivating product descriptions. This will often be the deciding factor that separates you from your competitors. In short, you need to make your descriptions as unique as possible and make your potential customer feel as though they can't live without your item. Here are a few key elements to include in your product description:

- Color
- Weight
- Size
- Desirable Features
- Maintenance Tips
- Special Deals or Discount Offers

This is your chance to really sell what you're offering to your customer. For example, if you're selling "Baseball Cards" then let potential buyers know why they should purchase from you and not from someone else. While this can be tricky at first, product description writing is something that can be mastered with enough practice. As a general rule of thumb, make them so catchy that you would probably end up purchasing the product if it wasn't yours.

Can You Make a Living Selling on E-Bay?

Right now, there are thousands and thousands of people making a living from items that they sell on E-Bay. While making a ton of money on E-Bay right away might take some time, it is certainly a possibility as long as you do the proper research to determine the most profitable items to sell and remain persistent. As long as you're selling the right products, for the right prices, you'll almost certainly will be able to earn enough money to supplement your current lifestyle or to upgrade it.

This is one of the main reasons why generating positive feedback on E-Bay is so important. As a seller, having good feedback will make or break your success. Make sure that you're honest about the products that you're promoting and make sure that you're delivering them on time and for reasonable prices. Continually doing this will almost guarantee that customers will leave you positive feedback on a regular basis.

Maintaining a Professional Image

In order to maximize profits, you want to make sure that customers are taking you seriously. The best way to do this is to make sure that you set-up the "right" business structure straight from the start which should entail being honest and accurate with your item descriptions, shipping items in a reasonable amount of time and making sure that your packaging looks professional.

This will enable you to establish trust and credibility with your customers and will give them the confidence that they need to purchase from you repeatedly.

Conclusion

You have to employ effective strategies to consistently make money on E-Bay. I know this because I've been successfully selling on E-Bay since 2003 and I am an E-Bay powerseller. A powerseller is a distinction that E-bay places on its members who consistently rank among the successful sellers in terms of product sales and customer satisfaction.

How do I maintain this consistency year after year? Simply by employing and executing my personal E-Bay selling strategies. I even have special names for these particular money making strategies. They are "Find a Thirsty Crowd Strategy", "Second Drink Strategy", "Micro Targeting Strategy", "Karate Chop Strategy", "It's Used But So What Strategy", "The Refurb Strategy", "The Big Profit Strategy" and "The Option Strategy".

You can learn about these strategies and how to utilize them to make a boatload of cash in my book entitled **The Secrets of Making $10,000 on Ebay in 30 Days** .

Chapter 4: How To Make Fast Cash through Amazon's Associates Program

Although most people have heard about Amazon's Associates Program, not many are aware how it works or how to make money with it. In short, it's one of the perfect ways that you can make fast cash and can lead to significant profits if performed correctly. In the subsequent sections of this chapter, we are going to cover the fundamentals associated with using Amazon's Associates Program to make money online.

Deciding on Your Topic

The first step towards promoting products is to choose a particular niche that you'd like to specialize in. If you don't know where to start, try choosing an area that you are most passionate about. At the very least, choose a niche or products that can sustain your interest. After choosing your niche, narrow down the list of products that you wish to sell in that particular niche. The smart way to narrow down your list is by determining the products that you wish to sell popularity, commercial viability and the amount of competition associated with selling them.

Promoting Products

If you're interested in earning as much money as possible, it is recommended that you set-up a website. This will provide you with all of the leverage that you need to successfully promote the products that you're representing. Here are a few tips to keep in mind when choosing a domain name for your website:

- **Memorability**: If people can't remember your domain name then it is likely that they won't ever visit in the first place. By making it memorable, you'll make it much easier for current and future consumers to find you.
- **Practical**: Avoid choosing a domain name based on the amount of cleverness it conveys. Instead, you should focus on making it keyword rich. This will help it be

picked up by search engines like Google, Yahoo or Bing much more easily.

Expect to pay about $10 per year for a domain name. Depending on which company you go through, you can qualify for additional savings by purchasing your domain for additional years. For instance, you can purchase a 4-year domain for $30 instead of a 1-year domain for $10. After buying a domain, you'll want to go ahead and host it.

There are several cheap and effective hosting companies out there that can provide this service for as little as $5 per month. Finally, you'll want to go ahead and choose a blogging platform so that you can go about promoting your products. WordPress is very reliable and tends to be the most sought after among Amazon Affiliate advertisers.

Signing Up For an Amazon Associate's Account

Probably one of the more attractive features about this money making method is that it's simple and it's free. Simply visit the official Amazon website, scroll down to the bottom of the page, and click on the direct link to the associate's section. Afterwards, you'll be required to type in some basic information about yourself including your name, phone number, address, and social security number.

Depending on how you'd like to get paid, you'll need to include your bank account's number and routing number. Only after you've gone through these steps will you gain access to the links and banners that will be used to promote specific products. Keep in mind that there may be a certain monthly threshold that you'll need to reach in order to have your funds released. Look this information up when you sign up.

Adding Amazon Product Links to Your Website

This is how you're going to get paid. To create your first Amazon product link, visit the central homepage of the associate's section of the site. Scroll down and glance at the left sidebar until you see a section which reads "Build-A-Link". Here, you'll be able to find individual products that you'd like to promote.

Choose the ones that you like by dragging them over into the toolbar or your "Favorites" menu.

Adding the link to your website or blog is equally as easy. With Amazon, you'll have a lot of control over the style and design of your link. As a general rule of thumb, stylize it to match your site. This also helps the link seamlessly blend into your content. Also keep in mind that you can choose to add promotional product banners to your website as well. Utilizing both methods can drastically increase the amount of profits you make.

Writing a Solid Product Review

Writing a solid product review is the key to succeeding as an Amazon affiliate. If you can make your followers feel as though they can't live without the product then you'll be that much closer to receiving a commission from a sale that you help make. Here are a few tips to consider when writing a review for Amazon products:

- **Descriptive Title**: Stay away from bland titles and use your imagination. Also make sure that your title is as descriptive as possible. Otherwise, you'll risk having visitors never read your product review in the first place.

- **Strong Opening Paragraph**: Your opening paragraph should be strong and "hook" your reader into wanting to learn more about the product being promoted. You could start off by asking a simple question as to why or how someone in their shoes would be able to benefit. On the same token, don't give too much away during the first few sentences.

Other Affiliate-Related Tips to Keep in Mind

As a general rule of thumb, it is always a good idea to purchase the product that you're going to advertise. And there are a few good reasons for this. For one, you'll be able to develop a feel as to whether or not the product is even worth promoting.

Secondly, purchasing the item will provide you with much more insight and knowledge that you can use while writing your review. This is why we mentioned that it could be very beneficial to you if you choose a niche as well as products that you are passionate about. And do keep in mind that reviews for products are scattered all over the Internet. You need to give visitors a reason to come to your website.

If you'd like to earn additional profits then you could also open up a Google Ad Sense account. While it may not generate a lot of revenue, it is simple enough to start and maintain.

Conclusion

Making Fast Cash as an Amazon Associate requires very little money to get started. The basic essentials include finding the niche and products that interest you, purchasing a domain name, creating a website or a blog that have vivid descriptions and reviews of the products that you are promoting, getting your website or blog hosted and driving traffic to it. That's it, it's so simple!

Chapter 5: How To Make Fast Cash Selling eBooks

When selling eBooks, you are selling a product that can provide you with residual income for years to come. This is probably why so many people are attracted to writing and selling them. Making money by selling eBooks on your own website isn't incredibly difficult. In fact, it's something that requires a relatively small amount of money to start-up and can result in sizeable profits.

Effective Passive Income Stream

For those who don't know, "Passive Income" basically refers to money being earned off a product that can be sold over and over again without exerting additional labor. Essentially with passive income you make money while you sleep. This is what selling eBooks provides. Since eBooks are downloadable files, you'll be able to distribute them over and over again, without worrying about inventory or stock.

Making Sizeable Profits

While selling one eBook might not make you rich, selling thousands of them can. And this is why setting up your own website and promoting and selling a plethora of commercially viable eBooks is essential if you want to make a ton of money.

Since you won't necessarily make all of your sales in one day, eBook profits are going to vary. For instance, today you may experience 50 downloads for your product and tomorrow only receive 2. While eBook profits aren't necessarily predictable, they can be sizeable and you can earn a nice amount of money if you understand the fundamentals associated with creating, marketing and selling eBooks. Let's discuss some of those fundamentals to ensure that you have success selling eBooks on your website or through other venues.

Proper Formatting - The Key to eBook Success

No matter how well written your eBook actually is, very few people are going to read it unless it has a captivating title, cover page, and proper formatting.

Before you even pick up a pen or sit down behind the keyboard, make sure that you have a solid understanding about how eBooks are laid out.

Your ideal goal should be to make your eBook look as professional as possible, far before your customer reads what is inside. On the same token, make sure that you include a captivating description of your eBook either directly on the cover or on the sales page. Believe it or not, this will immensely influence and persuade people who are considering buying your eBook to make a purchase.

Writing Tips - Creating Content That Sells

In order to separate yourself from the thousands of other writers who are producing eBooks on the same subject as you are, you need to create content that offers real value. You'll need to incorporate your organizational, research, and writing skills to put together a final product that consumers are going to love. Here are a few pointers to keep in mind when developing content for your eBook:

- Make sure that all of the information you're acquiring is up-to-date and relevant to the subject at hand.
- Thoroughly research the subject that you're writing about.
- Read as much information on your particular subject as you can. This will provide you with additional ideas when it comes time to actually write.
- Include links in the contact area of your eBook so that readers can visit your website or send you an email with feedback, questions, or concerns.
- Make sure that your content is original and re-written from your point of view to avoid being compared to similar eBooks on the market.

Making money with eBooks has become incredibly common and you'll definitely increase your profits once you learn how to write in the correct format. As a general rule of thumb, try to use Arial as your font type and 12 or 14 as your font size. While this isn't a concrete rule that you need to follow, it tends to be quite universal among the highest grossing eBooks currently available on the Internet.

Marketing your eBook

The easiest and best way to market your eBook is by having your own website. You'll want to create as much "buzz" around your product as you possibly can. The more people see it, the more likely they'll be to purchase it. You should develop a 500 word to 1,000 word sales/landing page for your eBook in order to hook consumers into buying your product.

Your sales page should be unique, captivating, and tell potential buyers everything that they should expect and will get when they purchase your eBook. A good technique to utilize would be to incorporate a "Chapters Section" in your sales page that demonstrates all of the chapters in your eBook as well as what they are about. This will provide buyers with a bit more information that they can use to make an educated decision about their purchase.

Conclusion

The idea of selling eBooks may sound challenging, but it can easily be implemented with a little patience and persistence. Remember that eBook selling is all about offering value to the marketplace. Offering a lot of relevant valuable information on a particular subject to a specific target audience will ultimately allow you to make continuous and consistent profits.

Chapter 6: How To Make Fast Cash Publishing Kindle Books on Amazon

Another incredible way that you can utilize to make Fast Cash is by selling Kindle books through Amazon's Kindle Direct Publishing program. This is another way to generate passive income for your pockets and you don't even have to be a writer to sell Kindle books. I will discuss how you can do that shortly, but for now I want to share with you some of the keys to creating and selling Kindle books.

Pick a Topic

Before you start writing anything, you need to pick a topic that your potential audience will find of value. Your topic should be in demand, and be something that you're completely comfortable writing about. It's quite likely that you're already an expert at something.

Simply find out what that something is so that you can start writing about it. There is no rule of the thumb on whether you should write fiction book or a non-fiction book. As I already stated it should be something that you're comfortable with. There are literally thousands of niches out there to choose from so you shouldn't be strapped to find the one that works best for you.

Browsing Through the Kindle Store

Upon browsing through the Kindle store, you'll immediately be bombarded with top sellers, recommended readings, and other suggestions that people are looking for. At first glance, this may appear as a bunch of random books. However, keep in mind that you can use this information to your advantage by seeing what type of books are popular which should aid you in making your decision on what type of book to write.

Writing Your Kindle Book

Just because publishing on Kindle is easy, doesn't mean that you're allowed to produce low-quality and unorganized content. Remember that Kindle readers are no less different than regular book readers in the sense that they want good material. If you start getting bad reviews because of a low quality produced book, you will sabotage yourself from taking advantage of this lucrative income stream. People will leave you bad reviews request refunds and you will soon be out of the Kindle book publishing business. The bottom line for success is simply this, make sure that you produce a quality book that readers will enjoy.

The book that you write doesn't have to be exceptionally long, but it should be formatted correctly and be free of grammar or spelling errors. If you want to know how to write a successful selling Kindle book, I have a book available entitled **The Fine Art of Writing the Next Best Seller on Kindle** that you will benefit from immensely.

How to Hire Someone to Write your Kindle Book for You

If you aren't entirely confident in your writing skills, or simply don't have the time to write, you can always opt to hire ghostwriters to handle this for you. Fortunately, there is a huge demand for writers like these and their pricing will range depending on skill and experience level. Here are a few of the more prominent websites that you could use to outsource the writing aspect of your kindle publishing venture:

- E-Lance
- O-Desk
- Guru
- Freelancer

Formatting Tips and Strategies

Every Kindle book that you write should have a clickable table of contents as well as a cover page. First off, make sure that your cover design is one that will really blow readers away. If it looks amateurish then you'll probably achieve amateurish results. Keep in mind that people are always going to judge a book by its cover.

Fortunately, there are several different places where you can have your cover design outsourced, and for a relatively small price. E-Lance, O-Desk, and Guru are all excellent and cost-efficient places where you can find freelance designers to design your book cover for you. The turnaround time is very quick as well, usually between 3 and 5 days.

Valuable Formatting Resources

There are a wide array of tools that you could download in order to successfully format and preview your book. The programs we are going to talk about are designed to provide you with the ability to preview your book before it gets downloaded. Here are some of the more popular formatting resources that you should consider downloading to increase your chances of succeeding with Kindle publishing:

- **Kindle Previewer**- Provides you with the option of previewing your Kindle book before publishing. This is quite useful as it will allow you to see whether or not you actually formatted it correctly.
- **Adobe InDesign Kindle Plugin**- This plugin is designed to make the entire Kindle book converting process much, much easier. In short, it will convert content into a single,

useable file that comes in both "Mobi" and "KF8" formats. It's a great option for those publishers who are trying to make their books work on a wide range of Kindle apps and devices.

Do You Need an ISBN Number?

In short, you don't need an ISBN number to publish on Kindle (despite what most people believe). Instead, you will receive something known as an "Amazon Standard Identification Number" which will basically be your book's unique number that will allow it to easily be found on Amazon. However, if you do have an ISBN number then you can choose to enter it when you are asked during the Kindle publishing process.

Uploading Your Kindle Book

Uploading your Kindle book is a rather simple process and all you have to do is follow the instructions in the prompts that you will be confronted with. The final part of the uploading process is clicking on the "Publish" button. Once you have done that it will take about 24 hours before your book is actually in the Kindle book store.

Royalties:

As a publisher, you'll be able to choose from two main royalty options: thirty five percent and seventy percent. In order to receive the latter option, you need to make sure that your book is priced anywhere between $2.99 and $9.99. Anything priced below $2.99 is only eligible to receive the 35% royalty rate.

Promoting and Marketing Your Kindle Book

Promotion and marketing are the keys to achieving Kindle Publishing success. In order for people to buy your book they first must be aware that it exists. The way that they will know that it exists is through the promotion and marketing of your book. There are numerous ways that you can promote and market your Kindle book and here is a list of a few:

- Virtual Book Tours
- Book Trailers

- Forums
- Blogging and Guest Blogging
- Getting Book Reviews
- Radio Shows and Podcast Interviews
- YouTube
- Press Releases
- Utilizing social media (Twitter, Facebook, Google+ etc.)

In my book entitled **How To Promote Market and Sell Your Kindle Book:** Amazon Kindle Publishing Marketing Promotion Guide, I extensively discuss these particular promotion and marketing strategies as well as others.

Conclusion

Making money selling Kindle books can be quite lucrative, whether you choose to write your Kindle book yourself or outsource the task. With such a massive and voracious market available, you'll be able to earn a steady stream of passive income.

Chapter 7: How To Make Fast Cash by Offering Small Services on Fiverr.Com

While $5 may not sound like a lot of money, imagine if you were fulfilling several hundred $5 orders on a monthly basis. Well, this is exactly what Fiverr.com was designed for. In short, Fiverr is a global online marketplace that enables you to offer tasks and services, referred to as 'gigs' for $5. You also have the ability to earn more than $5 when you become a top rated seller on Fiverr.

Offering your services on Fiverr can be a quick and effective way to put some fast cash in your pocket.

Overview - Making Money on Fiverr.Com

Fiverr is free to join and to become a seller all you need is a paypal account and an email address. Registering is quite simple, all you have to do is create a username and you are in business.

You can offer services on just about anything including writing, illustration, design, and other consumer-related tasks that require very little time and effort. For some people, making money on this relatively new website has proven to be quite lucrative. Here are tips that you should follow if you're truly interested in making a significant chunk of change on Fiverr.com:

- **Step 1: Setting Up**- First and foremost, you need to come up with a service that you're willing to offer on this site. Think of skills that you are particularly good at that don't require much time or effort. If you aren't sure about the types of services that you can offer then check out Fiverr.com for yourself to learn more about what others are offering. Once you've come up with a product or service, describe it in full detail in the details section of the gig.
- **Step 2: Promotion**- Once you have listed your gig, the next step is to promote your gig as much as possible. Although Fiverr receives a great deal of traffic from people who are looking to purchase small business services for just $5 it still doesn't hurt to

promote your gigs through social media and other mediums as well.

- **Step 3: Optimizing Your Gigs**- Make sure that you optimize and use the appropriate keywords so that people can easily find your gigs through Fiverr's search engine. When people order your gigs make sure that you deliver what they ordered fast and make sure that it is quality work because you want to receive great feedback. Receiving great feedback will enable you to get repeat customers as well as attract and gain new customers. Also Fiverr allows you to use pictures and make videos of the products and services that you are offering. Make sure to take advantage of these underutilized features. It will help to spruce up your gigs.

The maximum number of gigs that you're able to post is 20. As a result, you'll want to make sure that you're leveraging each one to the best of your ability. Try to focus on several different niches so that you can always have money flowing your way in the event that demand slows down for a particular niche.

Assuming that you've followed the tips just mentioned, it shouldn't be too long before you start making fast cash on Fiverr.com. Remember that you can earn a good monthly income from this website as long as you're offering a variety of unique, quality, services to the Fiverr marketplace. For example, if you can offer article writing services as well as Photoshop services then it's likely that you'll double the amount of money that you make on a regular basis.

Payments

You actually only receive $4 when someone purchases your gig as Fiverr deducts a $1 fee for being a middleman in the transaction. Paypal also takes a cut of the action when you withdraw your money out of your Fiverr account. For example, if 3 gigs were purchased from you the amount you will earn after Fiverr has deducted their fee is $12. When you withdraw this $12 from your Fiverr account into your paypal account you will receive a total of $11.76.

The one thing to remember about Fiverr is it takes 15 days from the completion of the gig before you will be allowed access to your funds to use in Fiverr or transfer to your paypal account.

Conclusion

Fiverr.com is a great place to make money fast and you don't have to be relegated to making just $5 a gig as Fiverr now allows you to offer additional services or upsells to your particular gig increasing the amount of money that you make per transaction. These upsells are referred to as Gig extras and you can make an additional $5, $10, $20, $40, $50, or $100 per transaction.

Chapter 8: How To Make Fast Cash Mystery Shopping

To put simply, mystery shopping is the process by which a person poses as a regular customer and evaluates companies based on their ability to provide good service. Also known as "Secret Shopping", mystery shopping can be quite lucrative and can even supplement your current lifestyle if you know what to look for. In the following sections, we'll talk more about how mystery shopping works as well as how you can make money doing it.

How Does Mystery Shopping Work?

Businesses love feedback and mystery shopping allows them to gain essential information that will increase the quality of their services. As a mystery shopper, your job would be to enter a store posing as a customer. From there, you would be required to acquire important information which includes the following:

- Amount of time it took to be greeted.
- Speed of service.

- The overall cleanliness of the store.
- The amount of compliance that employees have with the standards of the company (dressing in uniform, greeting, etc.)
- Whether or not they actually assisted you with your problems.

As a mystery shopper, you will be responsible for capturing this information and you'll be paid for it. Depending on what company you go through, you'll more than likely be paid several weeks after your session is over. Let's take a look at a few critical tips that you should keep in mind to ensure that you make a lot of money mystery shopping.

Tip #1: Never Pay to Mystery Shop

This is the number one tip that you should keep in mind when it comes to finding work. There are many ads that will promise you a spot as a mystery shopping, as long as you pay them an upfront fee. The majority of the time, these are scam companies who are trying to take your money. Any reputable agency will never ask you to invest your money to become a mystery shopper.

Once you've chosen your company, all that you need to do is sign up. Fortunately, there are dozens and dozens of companies to choose from. Each one offers their own rate of pay as well as offer you the opportunity to be a mystery shopper in several different stores. Also depending on the company, you can either sign up online or in person, and you may need to answer a few test questions (which likely aren't hard) in order to become registered.

Tip #2: Check for Opportunities Frequently

You should be checking for available opportunities on a frequent basis. Most agencies will send you mystery shopping opportunities via email describing the location in your area that needs a mystery shopper. Since they can fill up quickly, you'll want to make sure that you cash in on it as soon as possible. The first person to respond to these emails will usually be the person who gets awarded the opportunity to be a mystery shopper.

Tip #3: Treat it seriously

If you don't take mystery shopping seriously then it isn't likely that you'll acquire future work. So the bottom line is make sure that you adhere to rules and honor your commitment.

On the same token, you should educate yourself about the rules and procedures associated with mystery shopping so that you can perform better. For instance, 99% of companies won't allow you to bring kids to your jobs and you need to be a certain age in some instances. Before you think you can cheat the rules, remember that all stores are equipped with cameras that will be watching you every step of the way.

Asking For Bonuses

You shouldn't be afraid of asking for bonuses. There are some companies that would be more than willing to provide you with extra compensation for putting in additional work that wasn't required. Bonuses can be as little as a few dollars and be as high as $200 for any given session.

By asking for bonuses, you'll cut down the amount of money required on expenses like gasoline and food. Mystery shopping doesn't require that you spend a lot of time and it can prove to be quite profitable. Once you have finished with a mystery shopping session, make sure that you enter your data as quickly as possible.

In most cases, you'll be required to enter your session info into a secure website. Do this as quickly as you can and right after the session. Not only will you get paid faster but you'll also open yourself up to further opportunities later on down the road. As a general rule of thumb, try to enter this information no later than 24 hours after you have completed your mystery shopping assignment.

Getting Certified - The Best Way to Increase Profits

Were you aware that it is possible to become a certified mystery shopper? Yes, in fact, you'll be registered under the "Mystery Shopping Provider's Association" and be able to stand out from the crowd as a result. Having this certificate will benefit you greatly including getting paid more, being offered more opportunities to mystery shop, and even qualifying for more bonuses on a regular basis. But it isn't free. In order to acquire this certificate, you'll need to pay $15 to take the test (as well as pay for all of your study materials beforehand).

And that's for the "Silver" certificate. If you're going for the gold one then you'll need to pay in upwards of $100. However, as a general rule of thumb, having either one is fine and both will land you high paying mystery shopping opportunities. If you're truly interested in acquiring your MSPA certification then check out www.mysteryshop.org to learn more. Finally, don't expect to get rich from being a mystery shopper.

Conclusion

If you live in a highly populated metropolitan area then chances are good that you'll be able to receive a significant amount of money from mystery shopping. If you're truly persistent, and you get certified, it isn't unlikely that you'll be able to make over $20,000 per year "mystery shopping". Not to mention, it can be a lot of fun and prove to be a rewarding experience.

Chapter 9: How To Make Fast Cash Flipping Websites

Flipping websites is one of the top ways to make money on the internet today. A lot of savvy online marketers and entrepreneurs have figured out ways to turn this into a lucrative money-making business, often earning several thousand dollars per month. The idea behind flipping websites is quite simple to understand: you take a website, fix it up, and sell it for a significant profit.

Although this doesn't necessarily mean that you're going to become a pro, you can make random sales on a periodic basis and still earn enough to make it worth your while. In this chapter, we are going to talk about all of the tips, strategies, and things to know about flipping websites. By the end, you'll have enough knowledge to go out and do it yourself.

Creative and Unique Way to Make Money Online

Most people can agree that flipping websites is one of the more unique ways to make money online. But did you know that it can be the most profitable as well? Yes, in fact, website flippers have been known to make $10,000 in a single sale. While this may or may not happen your first time around, it is something that you'll eventually be able to achieve.

Basically, Website Flipping is the process of buying a website, improving it and selling it for a profit or you can also build a website from scratch and "flip it" for cash. However, do keep in mind that it is much more likely that you'll make money if you fix what's already been made rather than building a website from scratch.

The term flipping comes from the real estate industry and it was made popular by the hit TV show "Flip This House" on A&E TV. Let's take a look at the two main routes that you'll be able to take with website flipping:

- **Starting from Scratch**: As the name may imply, you'll simply build a website from scratch and attempt to sell it that way. While this can be a profitable decision, you'll want to make sure that the website is making a decent amount of money before you try to sell it. That way, you'll be able charge a higher price and make a significant profit.

- **Renovating an Existing Site**: With this option, your job would be to take a site which already exists and make it better. This could include changing the design, offering new incentives, and re-arranging content in a manner that makes it more appealing to visitors.

Which method is better? In general, it is a good idea to start with renovating an existing site, especially if you aren't too experienced with flipping websites. Just keep in mind that you'll need to purchase the website in order to do this.

An average site can cost anywhere from a few hundred to a few thousand dollars depending on how much money it is earning. If you have the funds, then make sure that you correctly invest in one that is going to help you make the most possible return on your investment. In the following section, we are going to spend some time talking about the steps associated with making your first purchase.

How to Purchase Your First Website

Purchasing your first website that you intend on selling can be quite exciting but you shouldn't allow your emotions to get the best of you. An educated decision needs to be made to ensure that you don't lose out on your investment. Here are a few considerations to keep in mind before purchasing your first website:

- How old is the website?
- Has it been blacklisted from any search engines?
- How much money is the website earning if any?

If you can't answer these questions on your own then there are services that will help you with them. Keep in mind that this isn't a decision that you want to rush. After all, you'll likely be spending several hundred dollars on your first website and you aren't guaranteed to make a profit on it without putting in a significant amount of work first.

Making an Existing Site Better

After you've purchased your first website, you'll want to take the steps necessary to make it look better. This is known as renovating and it should be taken very seriously. You should consider acquiring a more professional design, making the content better, and even optimizing it for search engines.

Overall, this is a process that can take some time but the rewards are high. Only after you've fully renovated the website should you consider placing it back on the market. If possible, try to get the site to generate money as this will make it much more valuable when it comes time to sell.

Selling Your Website

The final step of the process would be to actually sell your website which is a process in itself. First off all you'll need to show potential buyers proof that your site is receiving some sort of traffic to it.

Secondly, you'll need to show proof that you're making money with the site.

After these two areas, among others, have been confirmed, you'll want to negotiate your price. Although you may have a fixed price in mind, you should be willing to negotiate with your buyer in hopes of making the sale.

In the end, you may have to settle for a little less than your proposed price. But if you've managed to make it to this point anyway, it's likely that you're still making a relatively large profit.

Is Website Flipping Hard?

For the first time website flipper, website flipping may prove to be a little challenging. But you'll come to realize that it becomes easier as you spend more and more time fixing up existing sites. Remember that there is a huge market for new and existing websites alike. If you become good at this then you're virtually guaranteeing yourself income for years to come.

And always make sure that you do your due diligence before purchasing or creating a website to flip. Not only will this save you time, money, and energy, but it will also make the whole selling and renovating part that much easier. If you are searching for buyers then you should consider joining a website called "Flippa".

What is Flippa.Com?

Flippa.Com is a middleman site that will allow you to buy and sell websites for a nominal fee. While you don't necessarily need to go through this website to make sales, it does make it that much easier because it targets the audience or buyers that you are trying to reach.

Fippa.Com will provide you with all of the tools that you need to make your sale including a listing page that you can fill with critical details about your site. Here, you'll be able to include relevant stats, pictures, and monthly earnings of your site.

Conclusion

Website flipping isn't for everyone. This is one reason why we listed 9 different ways to make Fast Cash in this book. Fortunately, website flipping is something that can be mastered with enough practice. Remember that you can either construct your own website or renovate an existing one.

Both have their pros and cons and it is best that you take a stab at both of them so that you can fully learn about what to expect from the process. This is the only way that you'll gain the knowledge necessary for bigger sales.

By this point, you should have enough knowledge under your belt to successfully navigate the various money making methods in this book. Some of them are relatively simple to employ while others do require some work. Nonetheless, they all work and they can all provide you with nice profits as long as you remain persistent. Here are some ways that you can fully leverage the amount of money that you make:

- **Continue Learning**: The best way to succeed with the money making methods described in this book is to go out and continue learning about them. Search the web and find out how the experts are utilizing these methods to make money. In the end, you may come across a new strategy or two that can set you ahead of the competition.
- **Have Patience**: While money may not start flowing on the first day, you should expect to make profits quickly after implementing these techniques. Also note that certain methods in this book do take a bit longer than others. Set realistic expectations beforehand so that you don't lose faith in the process.
- **Work Hard**: These strategies aren't going to work on their own. They require that you formulate a plan and execute. As long as you work smart and stay disciplined, you should see significant profits. As a general rule of thumb, the amount of relevant work that you

put in will be directly correlated with the amount of money that you make.

Which Method is Right for You?

It is almost impossible to determine which money making method is right for you without trying them all out first. In fact, this is something that I highly recommend that you do if you'd like to earn the most amount of money possible.

Above all, it is important that you learn how to have fun and enjoy the process of making fast cash without having to work at a job. Good luck and go get em!

Other Books Available By Author Available On Kindle, Audio and Paperback

How To Create A Profitable Ezine From Scratch

The Secrets Of Making $10,000 on Ebay in 30 Days

The Complete Guide To Investing in Gold And Silver: Surviving The Great Economic Depression

How To Sell Any Product Online:"Secrets of The Killer Sales Letter"

How To Make A Fortune Using The Public Domain

Search Engine Domination: The Ultimate Secrets To Increasing Your Website's Visibility And Making A Ton Of Cash

Creative Real Estate Investing Strategies And Tips

How to Make Money Online:"The Savvy Entrepreneur's Guide To Financial Freedom"

How to Overcome Your Self-Limiting Beliefs & Achieve Anything You Want

The Secrets of Finding The Perfect Ghostwriter For Your Book

The Creative Real Estate Marketing Equation: Motivated Sellers + Motivated Buyers = $

How To Start An Online Business With Less Than $200

How To Market Your Business Online and Offline

Money Blueprint: The Secrets To Creating Instant Wealth

Affiliate Cash: How To Make Money As An Affiliate Marketer

Winning Habits: How To Cure Your Loser's Mentality And Turn Your Life Around

How To Promote Market And Sell Your Kindle Book

AudioBook Profits: How To Make Money by Turning Your Kindle, Paperback and Hardcover Book into Audio.

Money Magnet: How To Use The Laws Of The Universe To Attract Money Into Your Life

Conquering Your Fears

How To Master Your Emotions

The Fine Art of Writing The Next Best Seller on Kindle

www.ingramcontent.com/pod-product-compliance
Lightning Source LLC
Chambersburg PA
CBHW071622170526
45166CB00003B/1150